Say So!

I WILL! I CAN!

**OPEN
YOUR
*MOUTH!***

I AM!

Jeri Darby

Jeri Darby

ISBN: 978-1-958811-09-2

Ararity Press
jeri@iamawriternow.com
989 402-4721

Facebook: Jeri Darby (Personal)
Facebook: I Am a Writer Now (Author)
Website: https://iamawriter.now.site

LET
THE REDEEMED
OF
THE LORD
SAY SO!

PSALM 107:2

Dedication

This book is dedicated to:
Jesus Christ, who is the Author and Finisher of my faith.
The One who kept His commitment to *never* leave or
forsake me.

The Holy Spirit, my Comforter, Counselor, Personal
Assistant, and My *Very Best* Friend.

To the King, Eternal, Immortal, Invisible and the Only
Wise God, my Heavenly Father, Creator who is my Endless
Source and Sustainer.

PREFACE

*A*rise and shine! It is time to stop feeling like an imposter! Time to silence the voices assaulting your mind telling you that you are *NOT* enough! *NOT* good enough! *NOT* smart enough! *NOT* pretty enough! *NOT* talented enough! *NOT* … Tell the devil enough is enough! Stop comparing yourself with everyone! God wants to do something unique within you.

God is summoning people of all ages, all giftings, and all anointings, whatever your station in life —*to come forth!* Before you were tucked inside your mother's womb and launched into this physical realm, God sealed His plan and purpose within you! Release unto the world that which God deposited.

Decreeing His word aligns you with His plan for your life! There is power in your spoken words. Regardless of what others say—you and I must say *SO!* What are we to say? Whatever God has written in His word, whispered in our ears, or carved in our hearts— is *SO!* Every word He has spoken over our lives—is *SO!* Therein lies our victory! The power of life and death is in our tongues. Say *SO!*

My nursing background causes me to ponder things from a medical viewpoint. God could have said that the power of life and death is in the brain. This is a very significant organ, and when it flatlines, this indicates that life is no longer present. God could have said that the power of life and death was in the heart. This is a very significant organ, and when it is no longer beating, we know death has occurred. God could have said that the power of life and death was in the lungs. This is a very significant organ. When it can no longer perform its function of receiving oxygen and releasing carbon dioxide, death is imminent.

God chose to place the power of life and death within the tongue. This is the smallest organ of the body. Our tongue can release life—or death. It is not planted on the inside of our bodies as these other organs. When death is released, it is in our ability to correct this with words, without invasive medical procedures. Speaking life is a choice. You will notice in this book that "satan" or references to him are minimized by using smaller print. It is time that we divert the focus from satan onto the greatness of our God!

Oh! That we, the people of God, would live, act, and speak as though our spoken words have power! Stop allowing emotions, circumstances, or other outward influences to determine *what* you speak *when* you speak or *if* you speak. When difficult situations corner us, positive decrees may not readily flow from our lips. In such times, you may even battle to bring them to the forefront of your mind. You may get frustrated when positive words elude you. Get unstuck! This book will empower you. Rip off that satanic muzzle, toss it aside, and Say So!

When Moses asked God, who shall I say sent me? God responded I AM That I AM! That's how I have come to view my life and journey of faith. At any time, God can call forth any dormant seed lying within me, I AM THAT I AM. Whatever God calls me forth to be—*that I AM*! AND SO ARE YOU… I had the privilege to work with a remarkable man. When I met him, he was a social worker. Before he was a teacher, he went on to become a medical doctor and later a psychiatrist.

His compassion and professionalism impacted many lives in each of those arenas. Any one of those specialties could have become a lifetime role. He stepped into each with elegance and commitment and left a legacy before venturing into each new position. We are the children of the Most High God. No matter how meager or insignificant you feel your life has been, greatness resides within you. Make it your declaration today, *WHATEVER,* God says I AM, that I AM! With all boldness, all courage, all clarity—*SAY SO!*

YOU
SHALL DECREE
A
THING
AND
IT SHALL BE
ESTABLISHED
FOR YOU!

JOB 22:28

Table of Contents

INTRODUCTION

This book is designed to refill your decree reservoir and reset your mind while unmuzzling your mouth. It is time to declare the blessings of God, even when it does not *seem* feasible. Most of us have been taught the power of decrees. Yet, life can present circumstances that leave us speechless with gaped mouths! Have such times caused you to feel buried, cornered, or defeated? Have you ever felt like you were suffocated by fear to the extent that you could not think or respond to the presenting challenge with faith? Negative thoughts and feelings can overpower and swallow you like swarming darkness.

You know what you want to say, but the words are trapped in your throat. During times of desperation, satan attempts to snap a muzzle over our mouths. The last thing he wants is you shooting him with life-filled words laced with faith. he knows that as these words emerge from your spirit, flow through your lips, re-circulate through your ears, and stream back into your spirit, faith is fortified. I am writing this book in 2020, during the historical COVID-19 outbreak. We are yet anticipating its aftermath. This pandemic has plagued the world and ushered us into a new era. Life as we knew it has vanished! We need unshakeable faith in this hour.

Citizens are mandated by the governor to wear masks for protection of themselves and others. The mask is symbolic of what satan has been doing in the spirit realm for generations.

1

Even before this virus people have been wearing invisible muzzles. These demonic devices prevent the spoken release of God's promises from escaping your lips and disbursing into the atmosphere. Can't you feel it? Rip that muzzle off! Go ahead, do it as a prophetic act. Snatch it from your mouth and cast it into outer darkness! We have been redeemed by the Blood of the Lamb, and it is time to *Say SO!*

When God planted this book inside my spirit my excitement flooded! I rushed home during lunch breaks, settled into my secret place, and declared the written decrees included in this book. Soon rather than a joy, it became a chore until this practice suddenly ended. It felt like someone placed a padlock on my mouth and destroyed the key. Why does satan war so intensely to shut our mouths? Is it true that he is intimidated by the power of God's word targeting him? Can we really cause havoc in the kingdom of darkness by mere words? Yes! "For the weapons of our warfare *are* not carnal, but mighty through God to the pulling down of strongholds." (2 Corinthians 10:4 KJV) Words can form or destroy strongholds.

I have witnessed word power time and time again, yet there are times when there is a warzone inside me. Words flowing from my heart are barricaded inside my mouth, seeking an exit. These words struggle to break free, but my tongue is weighted and unable to speak. Invisible barriers trap them like hostages held at gunpoint for ransom, commanding their immobility. satan knows that once faith-filled words permeate the atmosphere, victory is imminent!

2

Battles are won or lost by our ability to destroy these barricades, imprisoning our words. Things shift in the spirit realm when we speak those things that are not—as though they were. (Romans 4:17) This is how it works in God's kingdom. For out of the abundance of the heart the mouth speaks. (Luke 6:45 KJV) The mouth empties that which is abiding in the heart. Our mind needs constant renewal to equip us to align our speech with God's.

While reading a list of word-based decrees or repeating them from a recording, God arises! This activates you to speak other decrees that He is releasing over your situation with power and authority!

I challenge the reader to not only practice the declarations that are written in my book—but also create an ongoing list. Boldly decree God's word over your life—daily—several times a day. *No!* Don't believe satan; he is a liar! You are not overdoing it. We cannot proclaim the word of God over our lives too much!

This is warfare! Let's fight a good fight of faith! Your words are your ammunition! Read your decrees into your phone recorder and listen as needed throughout the day or night. Integrate this practice into your life during good times and bad. It will fortify you to withstand life's most difficult moments with faith and victory. God is Faithful! Let the people of God arise and *Say So!*

I

Believe!

BELIEFS?

I was talking to a guy and it seemed we were making a connection in every way—*until*—we shared our spiritual beliefs. It was here we deadlocked. How can two walk together when they both are thinking the other is spiritually deceived? I was disappointed as I have been single for many years and was enjoying our pleasant conversations—*at first.*

Potential partners need to share at least foundational beliefs to have hope for a positive outcome. Anyone unwilling to consider that Jesus is the True Vine, the Door, the Truth, the Life, and the *only* Way is not someone that I am willing to entertain as a divine connection. This person was once a Christian minister and continues to minister in another belief. I Timothy 4:1 NIV says, The Spirit clearly says that in later times some will abandon the faith and follow deceiving spirits and things taught by demons.

satan loves to collect trophies. That's what you become once he has conned you into believing that Jesus never existed or that He was merely an ordinary man. You become a satanic mouthpiece denouncing the faith and aligning yourself with the agenda of the antichrist. he uses those who have *fallen away* to scoff and mock those choosing to pray, believe, and declare God's word over their lives.

Gross darkness is covering the earth. This is no time to be scuffling in confusion with everybody's doctrine. There are doctrines of men, doctrines of devils, and our own convoluted doctrines. The Holy Spirit is Faithful to lead and guide us into *ALL* truth if we surrender and listen. The problem is satan is skilled in the art of deceit. he succeeded in misleading a third of heaven's angels.

However, I don't invest energy in debating spiritual principles with others. The Bible tells us to be fully persuaded in our own minds—and people are! Even when their beliefs do not reflect God's truth. They are choosing a slippery path leading to destruction.

We all see and know only in measures and are all mistaken about some things. Everything that *can* be shaken—will be. In the end, only the unadulterated truth of God's word shall stand. I don't get it. Even as a child, I knew the Bible was no ordinary book. I didn't understand why adults couldn't see this. The words illuminated on the page as I read. I sensed a comforting presence inside me during Bible reading, and I knew that Someone special was watching over me.

Through the trauma of my troubled childhood, satan sought to uproot this foundation God was building upon His word. "Man shall not live by bread alone, but by every word that proceeds out of the mouth of God." (Matthew 4:4 KJV) This became my Rhema word at age nine. Once spiritual hunger awakens, spiritual darkness arises, seeking to appease and deceive. Whoever words you choose to pacify your spiritual craving, their plan is activated in your life. Many have feasted on the demonic bread of deception and have developed rigid mindsets, causing them to reject the truth of the gospel.

While shopping, I ran into a former high school classmate. I hadn't seen him in years. He shared that he had been ministering. "What church do you attend?"

He frowned and said, "I don't do traditional religion! I was in a cult for years!" He went on to explain that his brother was attending a cultic church. He was referring to a church where the pastor was a well-respected community member. "They do confessions that they are healed when they are not. Does your church do that?" This pastor and other congregation members had testimonies of supernatural healings from terminal conditions.

Wow! My mind spun. What are the odds that I would run into someone whom I haven't seen in years and engage in a conversation about decrees? This was the same week the Lord impressed upon me to write a book about declarations and confessions. I would *never* attend a church that did not believe in the power of confessing and declaring God's word. I considered my response carefully.

I answered, "I don't engage in spiritual debates. I believe that Jesus Christ is the Son of God, and I worship Him."

He looked at me and, following a brief hesitation, said, "Oh, okay," he spun and dashed away without another word. The Bible tells us to avoid vain babblings. (2 Timothy 2:16) When satan has others on scoffing assignments, it is not likely that they will receive anything you say. It can cause back-and-forth bickering that seldom produces positive fruit. The Body of Christ is experiencing shaking, uprooting, tearing down, and planting. Many are falling away. Though it should not be shocking because God warned this would happen. It is yet disturbing watching those once rooted and grounded in the word of God scattering onto diverse paths. People are embracing doctrines that completely disregard or even ridicule those of us clinging to biblical truths.

satan wraps false beliefs in half-truths, a tactic he has perfected since the garden. I can't imagine what lies he fabricated to deceive a third of heaven! Even if you must force the decrees from your lips—do it! It's amidst long seasons of silence that we experience our greatest losses. Become violent with the unmuzzling of your mouth to regain your freedom of speech.

I have included decrees that involve proclaiming your beliefs. Root and ground yourself in sound scriptural truths concerning the gospel. Know for certainty that Jesus is your Savior and the Author and Finisher of your faith. Jesus Christ is the Son of the Living God and there are no other means whereby men can be saved! Don't be wishy-washy with your faith! Take a stand for what and Who you believe!

SAY & SEE

"Come forth if you would like prayer, or to invite Jesus into your heart." The illuminating sermon about the love of God and the benefits of salvation left my heart throbbing and hungering for more. My body tensed and I held tight to my infant daughter. I did not have a lot of experience with prayer lines or attending church, and I had *never* witnessed anything like this! We were in a large tent on a huge lot off a busy street. Loud music blared and echoed throughout the neighborhood while some danced, some wept, some were waving their hands in the air. The minister placed his hand on the forehead of each one as the prayer line progressed. Some fell to the ground others began babbling words that I did not understand.

My place in line moved closer to receive prayer, and a woman reached for my baby. I shook my head in protest and squeezed her closer. I was confused and scared. Yet at the same time, I felt glued in the line progressing towards the minister to receive prayer. My life was in shambles. I had recently evaded my parent's home and moved into a tiny apartment. I was a depressed high school dropout and single mother trying to find her way. satan circled me while licking his chops, thinking, "Fresh meat!" God's grace drew me to this historical moment beneath the tent during this outpour of His power!

"If this is *really* God, He will not allow me to fall and hurt my baby," I thought. My turn came, and I stood face to face with the man of God. I don't remember his prayer, but he placed oil on his hands and touched my forehead while pronouncing words of life. Amazed, I did not feel a thing! My eyes swept over the crowd of dancing, crying, babbling people in confusion. I went home thinking that maybe the whole thing was a hoax. My transformation began immediately. That night, I was baffled because my cigarette tasted strange. I squashed it out and lit another—and experienced the same thing. My craving for nicotine left that night.

A sudden desire to go to church emerged, causing me to attend other services in the new church that Apostle Willie O. Coates, from South Bend, Indiana, planted in Saginaw, Michigan, the city in which I resided. That's how it works in the kingdom of God. We say and see.

True, the results are not always immediate, like my salvation story. At that sacred moment, I became a citizen of two kingdoms. The kingdom of this world and the Kingdom of Heaven. Things work differently in God's kingdom. To thrive in this new reality, I had to learn new principles. God's kingdom is built upon a foundation of words. Embracing this truth is necessary to experience the reality of His kingdom.

It was not until the man of God prayed faith-filled words of deliverance over me, and I repeated the prayer of salvation that I experienced a remarkable change in my life. These simple actions caused old things to perish and all things to become new. These changes were undetectable by the natural eye—they occurred in the spirit realm. Immediately, I was adopted into a new family, loved and accepted just as I was. I was planted into a spiritual kingdom that operates on spiritual principles—the most important being the law of *say and see*.

Years ago, a popular toy company produced a toy called *"See and Say."* Talk about durability; that thing was practically indestructible! The toy was created for toddlers learning to speak. Pull the string, and the dial spins and stops on a picture. A recording enunciates the name of the image the dial landed. The child makes the visual and auditory connection and repeats what's heard, thereby increasing their vocabulary. This was a great learning tool—for children. This pre-recorded device was a parental favorite for years.

God's kingdom often functions in opposition to the principles of this world. In His kingdom, those who give—receive. Those who humble themselves—are exalted. The first—are the last. He takes foolish things and confounds the wise. And most importantly, those who *SAY—SEE*. We activate the power of *SAY* and *SEE* using our tongues. Words do not discriminate. We will see what we say whether good or evil. Like the Apostle who prayed for me, and my life shifted right away, we can pray for others and believe in God for their redemption.

Though this is taught and embraced as truth, it is not practiced consistently. People speak the craziest things and follow it with, "Just kidding!" I can't count the times that I heard this response when attempting to warn someone about the potency of the deadly negative words they released. Face it—words are seeds. If we took a bag of corn seeds and scattered them onto the earth. Then say, "Just joking! I wanted tomatoes."

Guess what? *YOU ARE GETTING CORN!* It is the same with words. If you speak words laced with cynicism (even if *joking*), that's the harvest your words will produce. We habitually speak the lies of satan instead of declaring God's promises. satan's words are laced with doubt, fear, and unbelief. Once we agree with him, we fling doors open for him to strip the promises God desires to release in our lives. "We are snared by the words of our mouth." (Proverbs 6:2) If you are not releasing fruitful words—shut your mouth—*now!* This is no time for doubt, unbelief, nor cynicism. Regroup and rethink what you are saying! Decreeing the promises of God secures victory.

Our journey as children of God begins with our mouths. With our mouths, we confess our sins. With our mouths, we repent. With our mouths, we ask Jesus into our hearts. Those who pray prayers of repentance from their hearts experience Jesus intervening in their lives in surprising ways. The process of using our mouths to follow the instructions given to us in the Bible is foundational. Our eternal security is predicated upon our willingness to walk by faith and *say*— Before we *see.*

I BELIEVE DECREES!

I BELIEVE that in the beginning, God created the heavens and the earth!

I BELIEVE that my seed is MIGHTY upon the earth!

I BELIEVE that God has given me POWER over all the power of the enemy!

I BELIEVE that if I resist the devil, he will FLEE from me!

I BELIEVE that *GREATER* is *HE* that is in me than he that is in the world!

I BELIEVE that God will *FINISH* the good work that *HE* started in me!

I BELIEVE that God takes PLEASURE in my PROSPERITY!

I BELIEVE that *EVERYTHING* my hands touch *PROSPERS*!

I BELIEVE that God has *RESTORED* the years that the locust and the cankerworm have eaten!

I BELIEVE that I *CAN* do *ALL* things through CHRIST!

I BELIEVE that if I walk in the Spirit, I will *NOT* fulfill the lust of my flesh!

I BELIEVE that God forgives *ALL* my iniquities and heals *ALL* my diseases!

I BELIEVE that there is *NOTHING* too hard for God!

I BELIEVE that God will *NEVER* leave or forsake me!

I BELIEVE that God takes *PLEASURE* in the *DETAILS* of my life!

I BELIEVE that God is doing a NEW thing in my life and it springs forth *SUDDENLY!*

I BELIEVE that death and life are in the power of my *TONGUE!*

I BELIEVE that Jesus is the *SAVIOR* of the world!

I BELIEVE that God has *ANGELS* assigned to *PROTECT* me!

I BELIEVE that Jesus has prepared a *PLACE* for me!

I BELIEVE that God is my *VINDICATOR!*

I BELIEVE that God will honor me with long life!

I BELIEVE the sufferings of this present time are not worthy to be compared to the glory waiting to be revealed!

MY I BELIEVE DECREES!

I

AM

BREAKING THE CYCLE

While growing up my self-esteem was so low it dragged the ground like a shadow. "Blackie!" Was one of my brother's favorite insults hurled at me. This brother brutally abused me as far back as I can recall. My mother did not protect me. She was loaded with fear, insecurities, self-loathing, bitterness, anxiety, and depression. These toxic emotions embedded inside her over the years. These timidities infiltrated me throughout my childhood. The insecure, fearful, and rejected me just wanted to lurk in the shadows beneath a cloak of invisibility.

I witnessed craziness within my family, my neighborhood, and within the world that others seemed to turn a blind eye. Standing at the forefront with anyone for any reason was terrifying. I submerged my thoughts and feelings. I just wanted to be left alone! God began dealing with me as a child. I experienced His presence at age eight and learned to recognize His voice. As I grew older, I detoured. God was faithful to lead me out of deserts and wastelands to rescue me from paths of destruction each time.

God taught me to challenge, defeat, and evict the voices residing in my head. "You are ugly! You can't do anything right! You will never…" They were loud and disturbing and roared whenever I attempted to venture beyond my chains of limitations. My journey led to a nursing career. This role challenged me to grow and confront my fears. I felt like I was the size of a molecule in a world of giants, like in the movie titled *Honey, I Shrunk the Kids!* I persevered through the grace of God.

He led me to accept a position in the mental health field when my thoughts were, "This isn't for me!" It turned out to be the most loved aspect of my nursing career! I learned much about the negative impact of self-talk. I witnessed the power of self-fulfilling prophecies (words people speak that come to pass, whether good or bad) in the lives of my tormented clients. I discovered the power in my mouth and began to exercise the power of my tongue.

No one escapes satan's strategic and well-organized intent to kill, steal, and destroy. Not a single person! Read (John 10:10) Regardless of where vile words originate, they tend to pile inside. Then, like a repeating recording, play over and over and over, in our subconscious. Are you living out satan's destiny-destroying lies? That is why! *You* can break this self-debilitating and destructive cycle—with *your* words. Open your mouth!

Just when you think you have overcome negative thoughts, they are triggered by the images, words, or actions of others. Your faith falters, and your esteem flatlines. You suddenly feel angry, depressed, anxious, hopeless, or even suicidal. It's time to renew your mind with God's word—do it *daily*. Take an intentional action of decreeing His word over your life. It will disrupt destructive thought patterns. This is *not* a magic act. Don't decree positive words for a week and cut the practice because you haven't noticed any changes—*yet*. Your mind has years of stored negativity to override. Exercise the power in your tongue, and that power will increase. You *can* and *will* break this cycle— if you do not give up! Say so! Say so! Say so…and *say so again and again and again!* I wish I had learned this earlier in life.

The enemy will infuse your mind with hesitation and skepticism while you are speaking life to yourself. he is concerned because, for years, he has succeeded in convincing you to believe the opposite of what you are saying. It is time to break free of his lying delusions. Stand your ground! Stare back at that defeated person peering at you through the mirror. Yes, you! *That* person! The one who has been tormented and victimized by satan's brutal lies for years. You have the power to end it—with your tongue. Start today!

Harsh words may have been spoken over you during childhood. Perhaps you were in an abusive relationship that butchered your self-esteem. Maybe toxic words were spoken by parents, teachers, bullies, leaders, or even pronounced from your very own lips. Anyone with the ability to speak has the power to heal or kill with their mouth—that includes you! satan uses any willing tongue like a machine gun to splatter your heart with murderous words issued by him. It is time to unload—*reload*—and fire back!

"I am confident! I am successful! I am courageous! I am powerful!" I started declaring positive words over my life soon after becoming a mental health nurse. Usually, these were a list of decrees that I got from a book or recording. This was the beginning of the process of making declarations over my life. Later, I discovered audiotapes that I played during the night while sleeping. Upon awakening, I sensed an inner transformation. You can intensify your decreeing exercises. Intensification is wonderful!

What do I mean by intensification? When something intensifies, it becomes greater, stronger, or more extreme, according to the Macmillan Online Dictionary. You can intensify your decrees by engaging your five senses. Declare the promises of God using scriptures. Don't be rigid; explore ways to deepen the experience of using this vital defense.

Try sitting in a quiet place while listening to instrumental worship or warfare music during declarations (whatever suits your natural flow). This integrates the sense of sound while opening your mouth, allowing decrees to invade the atmosphere.

Be creative, make it fun! Say so! Assume a posture of power, and use a confident, courageous voice ignited by faith! Integrate joy, excitement, and anticipation into your voice tone, body language, and facial expressions while declaring. Play upbeat music and do a victory dance! This displays a picture of faith—to God— *and the* devil.

When looking into the mirror, say your decrees while staring into your eyes. This clarifies. *"Person in the mirror, I am talking to you! YES! YOU!"* Every word penetrates the heart of the person staring back.

When I first began doing this. I laughed! Couldn't help it. "Yeah, right?" I could read the thoughts of the woman glaring back. She was thinking, "You don't believe a word of that!" She was right, but it didn't stop me. Over time, something shifted. My self-image lifted. It was no longer something I tried to pick off the floor and wrap around me like a garment. I walked with my head up; I looked others in the eyes. Though fearful at times, I had strength to break the demonic chains when they tried to contain me.

Decrees do not have to be practiced in the same manner each time. You can record your decrees on a device and play it back. Listen while driving, bathing, applying makeup, shaving, getting dressed, doing housework, or while engaged in other activities that you can lend your ears.

Once done, you can listen to your voice, making declarations while falling asleep. This is preferable to falling asleep with the TV. Why not allow your spirit to fill with the sound of your voice repeating what God says about you? You can enter the realm of dreams with God's word resonating. This is a great way to increase your faith as it comes by hearing and hearing and hearing... the word of God.

Another way to sharpen the sense of hearing is to sit quietly and listen, following your decrees. "You are the King's daughter, and you are here for official business." I heard these words following prayer years ago. They rescue me when I am in a slump. Another time, while sitting in church, I heard, "You are my prized possession." It is one thing to read the word of God, and another when we hear God confirm it to us personally.

Write what you hear God say. Your Father is speaking. God is excited that you are allowing His promises to merge deeper into your spirit. Hearing God validating His word and His love for you does wonders with erecting faith and erasing lies. Yes, satan will be right there screaming, *"That's not God!* That's what you *wish* God would say to you!" *Lies! Lies! Lies!* God is love. He is forever trying to convince us of His love! He desires to flood us with Everlasting love. Refuse to believe satan's deception. Listen, write, believe, and cherish God's spoken words to you. Hide them within your heart.

Integrate the sense of touch by placing your hand over your heart, head, or stomach in an affirming manner while decreeing. Our body has memories. Use your own gentle touch to integrate your declarations in a deep, affirming manner. Allow God's word to give you a spiritual *massage* while releasing pent-up frustrations from your spiritual muscles. This is a time to speak life to yourself. Life can be traumatizing, and we internalize tremendous pain.

Experience the power of these word exercises. You will feel your heart responding in a positive manner. Healing can begin with your very own words. Place your hand over your heart, insert your name into the blank, and repeat—aloud. I will give examples of each.

____(Your Name)____ I love you. (Say three things you love about yourself (nothing negative!)

Love

Jeri, I love you. You strive to see the best in others. I love that about you.

Jeri, I love you. You are determined and never give up on your pursuits. I love that about you.

Jeri, I love you. You are willing to examine your heart and practice walking in forgiveness. I love that about you.

Gratitude

Say three things you want to thank yourself for. ___(Your Name)___ (no ifs ands or buts). I will provide examples.

Jeri, you make the effort to connect with others in meaningful ways. Thank you for that.

Jeri, you are committed to hearing and following God's plan for your life. Thank you for that.

Jeri, you try to do the right things for the right reasons, even when others don't always understand. Thank you for that.

Appreciation

End with three things you appreciate about yourself,

___(Your Name)___ Stay positive! This is a powerful exercise! Examples to follow.

Jeri, you forge ahead in the face of doubt and uncertainties. I appreciate that.

Jeri, you habitually challenge yourself to move outside your comfort zone. I appreciate that.

Jeri, when you feel that you have heard God speak, you act. I appreciate that.

Do feel the impact of your positive words stirring your heart? Practice daily. Lots of things transpire on a spiritual level with this simple exercise. You will feel love, self-forgiveness, and confidence rising. Of course, do more than three or more often than daily if inclined. Often, we struggle to voice positive things about ourselves. Had I asked you to speak about your dislikes, perhaps you could have gone on and on. Self-love and affirmations aid in the healing of heart wounds. Post scriptures and decrees or purchase décor with life-giving words. Integrate them into your living and workspace where they are readily visible. Find moments when you can depart from BUSY and still be yourself. Meditate on God's promises and experience His reality!

There were times when I experienced a sweet taste, smelled roses, saw smoke, felt His words fall upon me, or sensed spiritual water engulfing me while stilling myself in the Lord's presence. Decreeing His word and pressing into greater levels of intimacy heightens your spiritual senses. His love has embraced me like a comforting blanket. God deals with us individually. The Bible says, "Taste and see that the Lord is Good." (Psalm 34:8 KJV) I can personally confirm this, for I have tasted His goodness. Allow Father God to surprise you!

IT WORKS!

A series of tragedies left me depressed, hopeless, and suicidal during my adolescence. I dropped out of high school in the twelfth grade—in the middle of midterms. A life of childhood physical and emotional abuse stole my voice, but I discovered the power of the pen. I loved the written word! I was shy and quiet and discovered that writing was a way to express myself freely. As a child, I dreamt of being many things. These aspirations were usually media-driven. While watching the popular series titled *Bewitched,* I wanted to go into advertising like the husband of the show's star.

When watching movies about espionage, I wanted to be a spy. I was young and impressionable and loved books. These childhood notions vanished with age, and I remained an avid reader. Reading was my means of escaping the trauma of my horrific childhood. Then, I decided I wanted to be a writer. Something inside me screamed, "You can do this!" I journaled through my high school years. During college, instructors offered frequent positive feedback about my writing assignments.

"Great job! Can I have a copy?" And similar comments were scribbled on returned papers. Poetry was natural for me. Other students requested me to write poems for their English classes. When someone was honored in church, I transcribed and read poetic expressions about their life and contributions. For years, I desired to write more, but I was clueless. I didn't know where to start! satan ridiculed me for having the audacity to think that I could ever become a *real* writer! My desire to write was scrutinized by him to the degree that after a while, I felt it was an unworthy pursuit—compared to those of others. satan convinced me that writers were of little importance. I started feeling like an undercover fraud.

satan assaults anyone who dares to profess that they are gifted at *anything*—especially writing. he was defeated by God's written word! he witnessed firsthand how God inserted Himself inside a book, and for over two thousand years, God's word continues to dismantle his kingdom strategically. At this point, I had not written anything beyond personal journaling and college papers. After my failed marriage, I began writing a book for singles.

In my forties, I heard God clearly speak, "Start telling others that you are a writer." This was a challenge. The next day, I walked briskly to the exit following the church service. I am not one to linger when service ends. This day, I engaged in conversation with a minister. "I am starting a Christian newspaper.... I will need submissions," is how our chat ended. Don't know how our conversation gravitated to writing in the first place.

"I am a writer!" I spoke aloud for the first time. Blurting these four words launched my writing career. *Saying so…* is empowering! Something happened in the spiritual realm. It was like the writing mantle descended and shrouded me from that day forth. I stepped into my purpose and destiny with fresh clarity and determination. I internalized their reality, and my inner author was unleashed. Holding onto this identity demands continual warfare. Regardless of what it is, satan will attempt to strip your God-given purpose and identity. *Standfast!*

I continued working sporadically on my first book, *Stepping Stones, Reflections for Singles,* and informed God that I had no idea how to move forward. "I will always have someone to help you continue with your journey whenever you are ready." Reassured by His promise, I engaged in magazine writing as writing articles felt less intimidating. I weathered the storm of frequent rejection letters piling in my mailbox.

"I need help!" I soon recognized and started attending conferences and workshops to become familiar with the publishing process. I learned how to follow submission guidelines and work with editors. Time and money invested during this season were invaluable. Applying strategies acquired through ongoing learning and online research soon paid off. Checks begin replacing rejection notices.

I enjoyed writing for magazines and became quite comfortable. When we are reluctant to press beyond the familiar, God will appoint someone to beckon us to journey further into the unknown. Such a person emerged. This woman approached me for several years, asking, "Jeri, have you published your book yet?"

"No, not yet." Was my repeated reply. I dabbled with it on and off over the years.

Jeri, if you finish your book this year, we can have a book signing together. Her persistence challenged me. I committed and completed my book. As God promised, he had someone there when I was ready. With patience, she guided me through the process of self-publication. After self-publishing several books, I began sharing advice with others who were desiring to publish. Again, I nestled into my zone of ease.

While praying for me one day, my mentor said, "God, we thank you for that publishing company." This was perplexing. This generated a God-directed silent response from me, and I did not hear another word she said.

"God, I did not ask for a publishing company. I don't want a publishing company!" My mind calculated that this was an impossible feat—*for me*. I could never accommodate such a huge assignment, and I concluded that I did not want any part of it! I thought the matter was settled. A few months later, following church, while walking towards the door, a woman intercepted my exit.

"Jeri, do you publish books? I had a dream, and God told me to talk to you. I need help with my book." Beyond offering advice and self-publishing my own books—I had done nothing major. I knew God was presenting me with an opportunity to step into purpose, and I agreed to help her.

This was my first client and the beginning of my journey as a Writing Coach. Annette Carnes is a seasoned woman of God and a gifted storyteller. It was an honor to help her publish not one but two books. It is a privilege to assist seniors with releasing their creative works. Countless writers die with untold stories. Powerful tales ripe with the miracle-working power of God enter the grave with them. I was sixty-two years old when I finally published my first book. Too many never experience the joy of caressing their creative endeavor because they failed to "work while it's day." God helped me to understand that this saddens His heart.

"I am a writing coach!" From time to time, I proclaimed this to others with reluctance. One night, I dreamt that someone asked me what I did. "I am a writing coach," I said and followed with gibberish, attempting to explain the services I offered. God and the angels watched while shaking their heads. Breaking the silence, God spoke and said, "She's got to have more confidence than that!" From that day on, I lift my head, make eye contact, and proclaim that I AM a Writing Coach with clarity, courage—and confidence!

Today, I know that I am walking in His purpose. I am anointed to A-Activate, I-Inspire, and R-Release the writer inside those God is calling forth to be authors. The Holy Spirit taught me how to empower others using those three words. Then He instructed me to take note of what their first letters spelled, A.I.R.- air. My coaching services remove the struggle and confusion for writers by releasing a surge of anointed fresh air to those I serve.

Watching a new author embracing their book for the first time brings me great joy. Many stepped onto their awaiting platforms to release the glory of God through their stories. The power of declaring *"I AM"* over your life is amazing and ripples through the sea of humanity! How far? Only God knows.

These are two examples, but there are numerous times that I have had to say—*before* I saw. God is faithful. He has done the exceeding and abundant and exposed satan as the liar and deceiver he is! Not only did he establish me as a writer, but he has utilized me as an instrument to release others struggling to soar into their author's identity.

Today, I have over a hundred publishing credits for articles and poems in magazines, three anthologies, and nine self-published books, with two translated into Spanish and offered on audible. I have set a goal to write one hundred books before I depart Earth.

I have a growing list of published authors who have benefited from my *I AM a Writer NOW!* Coaching Services. Even with sparkling book reviews and life-changing testimonials by others validating the impact of my coaching approach, satan yet dares to challenge my identity. The fight to maintain your purposed station in life is a never-ending battle! Adorn yourself with the armor of God and continue to stand in your God-given identity.

What has God whispered instructing you to declare over your life? Speak it into the atmosphere *TODAY!* I AM decrees are effective in suppressing the cruel, accusing voice of satan—who takes pleasure in watching you struggle to discover your identity. he is forever declaring what you are *not.* Has God confirmed in your spirit who you are? Decree it! If not, one thing we can each decree is we are the Sons and Daughters of the Most High God. Start there...

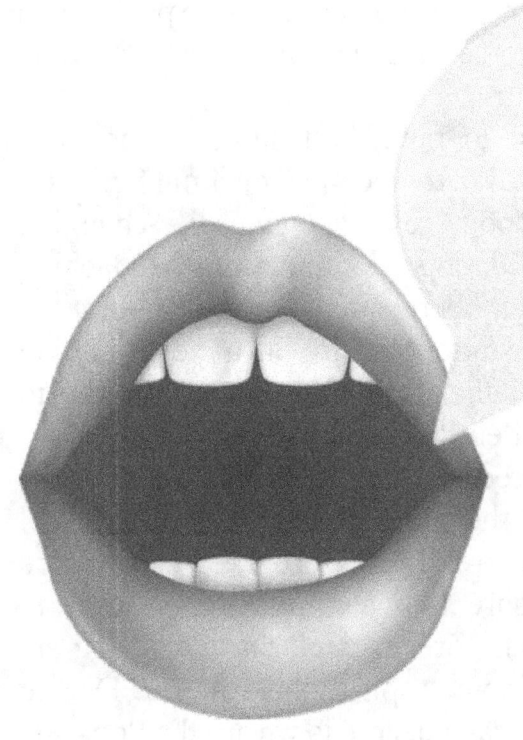

I AM DECREES!

I AM _Your Name, (Son/Daughter)_ of the Most High God.

I AM the HEAD only.

I AM blessed on my job and in my business.

I AM blessed going and coming.

I AM willing and obedient.

I AM filled with the Spirit of God.

I AM the RIGHTEOUSNESS of God in Christ.

I AM virtuous.

I AM a MIGHTY person of valor.

I AM healed.

I AM a peacemaker.

I AM the light of the world.

I AM walking in the plan of God for my life.

I AM a righteous seed.

I AM a generation of them that seek Your face.

I AM anointed.

I AM filled with purpose.

I AM so loved by God.

I AM set apart for the Master's use.

I AM God's bold witness.

I AM God's Masterpiece.

I AM God's prized possession.

I AM powerful through Christ.

I AM a TRUE worshipper.

I AM victorious.

I AM filled with witty ideas and creative inventions.

I AM pure in heart and living an abundant life.

I AM surrounded by people of wise counsel.

I AM well able to possess the land.

I AM protected by the Most High God.

MY *I AM* DECREES!

_____

_____

_____

_____

_____

_____

_____

_____

_____

_____

_____

_____

_____

_____

_____

I

Can!

DARE TO DREAM!

Soft-spoken, mild-mannered, loner, slow to anger, peacemaker, wish I were invisible—that was me! Not the greatest persona for a registered nurse. "I am going to nursing school," I announced to my family one day. They laughed! I dropped out of high school in the twelfth, obtained a GED, and no one in my family had attended college—*yet.* "You have never taken care of sick people! You will probably faint if you see blood!" My siblings taunted, and their words struck me like bricks.

"I *can* be a nurse!" My spirit protested. Their teasing ignited a fire inside. In silence, I determined, I *can* achieve this goal, I will prove them wrong if it's the last thing I do!" **Through** the grace of God—*I did.* Challenges emerged in many forms during this pursuit. I completed a Licensed Practical Nurse program and a few years later graduated as a Registered Nurse. When I finally finished, others saw my quiet mannerisms as weakness.

"You will do well, but you will need a strong nurse manager as a role model." One instructor warned before my RN graduation. Was this ever the truth! Following completion, I landed in a workplace filled with nurse piranhas. Knowing how to fend for oneself was a must! Showing kindness is important to me. Co-workers took my kindness for fragility—*wrong!* Over the years, I have learned to assert myself while guarding my heart. There will always be at least *one bitter, vindictive, insecure person who* singles you out in the workplace. Learn, grow, and move on stronger and wiser was my motto. I endeavored not to allow anyone's toxic behaviors to become duplicated and demonstrated through me. I practiced guarding my heart.

My desire was to work in the OB-GYN Unit where babies are delivered day and night. Can you imagine witnessing the miracle of birth routinely? I don't know where you plan on working, but you should really consider mental health!" One instructor recommended it. She witnessed my interactions with the mentally ill while completing the mental health portion of my RN rotation.

"Not for me!" I thought. I was terrified on my first day on the unit. Soon, it became a natural flow. After graduation God navigated my employment path into the mental health field— *I loved it!* The onset was rocky. I started working with a cliquish group that had been together for a while. My low-key approach did not suit them, and they constantly complained to our unit Charge Nurse named Karen Brisbois. Karen started approaching me with one complaint or another that they reported to her. I am thankful for her wisdom. She was a great observer and listener. Several times, she shared their concerns while allowing me to express the rationale of my approach.

After calmly explaining my actions. "Oh, okay." Is all she would say… *Until the next time.* This happened on several occasions. Karen was always impressed with the logic behind my decisions. One day, she stopped me, saying, "I am taking the position of Nurse Manager, and I would like you to take my Charge Nurse position. It's like she saw the faltering thoughts circling inside my head. "Don't answer now; think about it for a couple of days."

Wow! These thoughts raced in my head, "There is *no* way that I will take the responsibility of running this unit! Especially not with this crew!" I was a natural at mental health nursing; it demanded a level of courage, calmness, and confidence that I never knew I possessed.

"They are just people" is how God soothed my anxieties about working with His population with emotional disturbances. "They just want to be treated with respect like everybody else." Using this logic, I was effective in calming violent clients and often preventing physical altercations by convincing clients to take their medication before demonstrating explosive behaviors.

I was confident in my verbal skills, but being responsible for an entire unit? *What ifs* swam back and forth through my mind. God suppressed the doubt and fear enough for faith to arise allowing me to step into this new role weighted with new obligations. After wrestling with this commitment for a few days, I approached Karen and said, "yes."

Karen was elated. "You will be fine, and I will be here if you need anything!" I could see that she was genuinely happy for me. Karen is one of the most, confident, courageous, assertive, and innovative nurses that I have ever met. Though I have lost connection with her over the years, her mentorship imparted much strength, wisdom, and knowledge which I rely upon to this day.

I served in this role for ten years, left and returned, and completed two more. *"I Can!"* Manifested repeatedly during these ventures. Frequent daily crises demanded immediate decisions risking dire outcomes for all involved if unwise. God continues to stretch me beyond my faulty beliefs. I am grateful that the Holy Spirit sealed the "*I can* in my heart for each defining moment.

The Bible says that we go from strength to strength, glory to glory, and faith to faith. (Romans 1:17) Once we experience the faithfulness of God in one area, this gives us faith to trust Him in the next. Over the years, we look back and discover we have established history with God. This history arms us with the confidence that God will not leave us hanging. We have learned that He will cause us to triumph in the face of what to us—*seems impossible.*

God will only challenge us to the degree of the giftings that He has placed inside. What buried talents are withering inside you today because you never dared to say *I CAN!* Ask God for clarity, confidence, and courage. Then, *whatever* He says, do it! You *can* do all things through Christ! (Philippians 4:13)

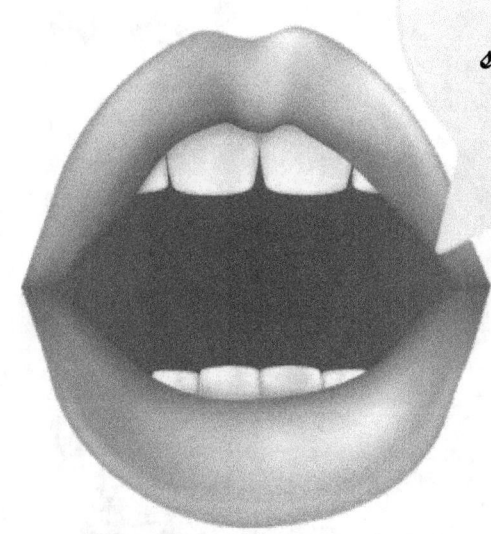

I CAN DECREES!

I CAN do all things through Christ Jesus, who strengthens me!

I CAN run through troops and leap over walls!

I CAN speak to mountains, and they are removed!

I CAN lay hands on the sick, and they recover!

I CAN follow peace with all men!

I CAN pray without ceasing!

I CAN rejoice in the Lord always!

I CAN create wealth!

I CAN discern spirits!

I CAN give thanks in everything!

I CAN bless the Lord at all times!

I CAN speak as the oracles of God!

I CAN be strong in the Lord and in the power of His might!

I **CAN** forgive them that trespass against me!

I **CAN** love my neighbor as myself!

I **CAN** go into all the world and preach the gospel!

I **CAN** be His witness!

I **CAN** hear and obey the voice of God!

I **CAN** endure hardship as a good soldier!

I **CAN** worship God in Spirit and in truth!

I **CAN** walk by faith!

I **CAN** humble myself under the Mighty Hand of God!

I **CAN** wait on the Lord!

I **CAN** study to show myself approved unto God!

I **CAN** acknowledge God in all my ways!

I **CAN** trust in the Lord with all my heart!

I **CAN** seek first the kingdom of heaven!

I **CAN** delight myself in the Lord!

I **CAN** break generational curses!

MY *I CAN* DECREES!

_____

_____

_____

_____

_____

_____

_____

_____

_____

_____

_____

_____

_____

_____

_____

I
Will!

INNER VOWS

My marriage ended. I cried, vomited, and had diarrhea for three days after making this decision. Not because I was in love but because the realization that I had wasted *ten years of my life* in a tortuous marriage to a man I didn't love was weighty. After the third day, I dried my eyes and declared to myself, "*I WILL never cry again!*" I didn't for over fifteen years.

To realize how peculiar this was, you would have to understand how readily tears flowed from my eyes and heart beforehand. Here are examples. If one of my children answered when my friend called asking, "What is your mother doing?"

"She's crying."

My friend would laugh, saying, "She must be watching "Little House on the Prairie!" Everyone knew that during that show, my tears flowed like clockwork. Another example: As a youth minister, I was mocked and called "Jeremiah, the weeping prophet," referring to the prophet who was noted for weeping for the nation's sins. Merely thinking about the unsaved evoked streams of tears. That definitive moment when I spoke, "I will *never* cry again," activated the power of my words and shut down my ability to cry—*for years!* Even when I wanted to—I couldn't. When pain speaks, we may not always like the aftermath.

Situations that bought joy, sorrow, and sadness when I longed for tears to mark these deserving moments—*nothing.* Gone were the days of weeping while watching emotional movies. *Why?* Because—*I SAID SO!*

I missed my God-given ability to weep. I once worked in the Crisis Department of my city's local mental health facility. One day, while assessing a woman in distress, tears streamed unimpeded from her eyes like a faucet flowing full force. It had been *years* since I shed a single tear. I was mesmerized by her ability to cry effortlessly.

While captivated by her heaving chest and noisy sobbing, I handed her tissues. Years of being deprived of the ability to cry left me feeling hard-hearted and cheated. "I silently prayed, "God, *please* restore my tears." No one wants to experience weeping arising from constant pain. But tears are a gift of sorts and capture God's attention.

The Bible says that God places our tears in a bottle. (Psalm 56:8) That tells me our tears have significance—even to God. I imagined my near-empty bottle of tears sitting next to this woman's. She has likely wept enough to fill an entire row of bottles just during our interview!

My tearless journey is a powerful illustration of the power of my mouth. My words released years ago stretched into my future, performing actions that I deeply regret. The long-lasting impact of yielding my voice to my pain is ever with me. Right down to an eye condition of chronic dryness. I relate this to the deficiency of tears released from them over the years. Can you understand why I have come to respect the power of the tongue? How many other things, whether good or bad have been spoken into existence and perhaps gone unnoticed? What's operating in our lives that we unknowingly set in motion with our tongues—even as children?

Inner vows are often spoken during childhood. We all have likely decreed things to ourselves and/or others as children or adults using sayings including words like *never* and *always.* The Holy Spirit has helped me reverse and cancel some childhood inner vows that were ruling my adult life. I am certain that there are more, and I trust that they will continually be revealed in time. I thank God for the Holy Spirit. He is committed to leading us to the truth. There are times when the Holy Spirit has identified an inner vow I made during childhood.

This insight usually follows circumstances resulting in frustration and impulsive actions. The Holy Spirit asks, "When did you decide to respond to this situation in that manner?" When I allow Him to trace the root of my behavior, a wounded, angry, and bitter child stands at the other end. The Holy Spirit has helped me to remember the age and situation, justifying my childish behavior. My acts were perfectly ok—*for a child,* but irrational as an adult. This question follows, "Would you allow a ten-year-old child to make that decision for you today?"

"Of course not!" With the guidance **of** the Holy Spirit, I am learning to recognize and abolish behaviors that are not conducive to adulthood. I am not the only one. These situations are more common than you may think. Our pain loves to speak. It will control your voice to make decrees over your life that you may suffer for in future years. Reclaim your tongue, redirect your pain to proclaim the promises of God! *Whatever* He says, *Say so...*

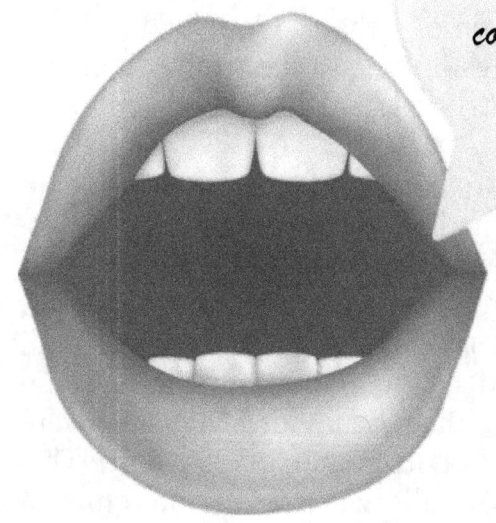

I WILL DECREES

I WILL decree a thing, and it SHALL be established for me!

I WILL seek the Lord while He may be found and call upon Him while He is near!

I WILL bless the LORD at ALL times; HIS praise SHALL continually be in my mouth!

I WILL say of the Lord that He is my REFUGE and my STRENGTH, my God. In Him, my heart does safely trust!

I WILL pray WITHOUT ceasing!

I WILL be strong AND courageous!

I WILL ENDURE hardship as a good soldier!

I WILL meditate on the word of God DAY and NIGHT!

I WILL say CONTINUALLY let the Lord be Magnified, He takes pleasure in my prosperity!

I WILL PROSPER and be in HEALTH even as my SOUL prospers!

I **WILL** offer unto God the SACRIFICES of praise!

I **WILL** HUMBLE myself in the sight of the Lord that He may EXALT me in due season!

I **WILL** BELIEVE on the Lord Jesus Christ as the scripture has said!

I **WILL** LOVE the Lord my God with all my heart, with all my mind, with all my soul, and with all my strength!

I **WILL** put on the whole armor of God that I will be able to stand against the wiles of the devil!

I **WILL** THINK about things that are pure, lovely, true, honest, and of good report.

I **WILL** SPEAK the TRUTH in love!

I **WILL** owe no man nothing except to LOVE!

I **WILL** follow PEACE with ALL men!

I **WILL** fear no evil!

I **WILL** SING a new song unto the Lord!

I **WILL** love the Lord my God with all my heart, with all my mind and all my strength!

MY I WILL DECREES!

I

Desire!

THE RIGHTEOUS SEED!

My children were school-aged when I uprooted them from church. Big mistake! There were generational repercussions for this irrational act. I am a mother of four. My fourth child was born during this churchless season. Thank God the Holy Spirit navigated me back to my Father's house when he was eight years old. His life was spared the devastation of his older siblings. Each one faced challenges with drugs, alcohol, and other diabolical obstacles.

My oldest son, Jimmie, took my exodus from church the hardest. Drugs and alcohol dragged him to the brink of death. "If you continue to drink, you will die." Doctors warned each time before releasing him from the hospital. He pledged to do better and continued to drink worse than ever once released. Fits of rage, anger, and rejection demolished our relationship during his early teens. Nothing I did was good enough.

He tagged himself *"least loved"* and flashed this label like a war hero's medal. He did not feel I or his siblings loved him—or maybe not as much as we loved each other. During family gatherings, everyone knew that his tolerance for group interactions was fifteen minutes—*or less.* He knew it was time to make a quick exit when he began to pace, fast talk, and lash out at everyone. Sometimes, he managed to depart before smiting everyone with his anger. Over the years, he began to opt out of invites, leaving the family with mixed feelings. Relieved because we escaped an angry episode, and regret wishing things could be different.

We rarely talked on the phone, and when we did, it was brief and cordial. Even during phone conversations, his inner turmoil was a smothering hopelessness seeping through, taking my breath away. "Say a prayer for me, Mom," he sometimes concluded our sporadic chats. My prayers declared the promises of God over His life, the promises that God extends to the seed of the righteous. I decree the blessings of God over my children, my children's children, and my children's, children's children. When I am long gone, my prayers and declarations will hover and descend upon them at the appointed time.

One day, I sensed the spirit of death lurking to claim him. While searching for his insurance policy, I became angry at the devil! "God, I so hate him! The havoc that he has inflicted upon this family is unforgivable. I hate him!" Now he was attempting to snuff the life of my son. My son, who was killing himself trying to medicate his satanic-induced misery with alcohol and drugs.

satan despised the great light God placed within Jim, it shone even from the womb. His love for others is profound. In his early adult years, he gave his heart to Jesus. During this brief encounter, Jimmie engaged in long periods of interceding; he loved prayer and praising God. He devoured God's word and became a walking Bible. When he strayed, he continued preaching even though he was rambling, stumbling, and drunk. He yet declared God's word to anyone who would listen. My heart desired to see him free. I prayed long years with stubborn faith whether at work or home.

A group of Christians on my job united and started a bi-monthly lunch prayer meeting at a local coffee shop. We gathered prayer requests and shared devotional readings. One day, a woman requested prayer for her son. Then she said, "I just remember the scripture Jeri shared, and I have been praying that."

"What did I share?"

"You said the seed of the righteous shall be delivered!" This scripture is found in Proverbs 11:21.

"Oh, I am going to pray that too." I share many things during our prayer group, and this slipped my mind. I had professed this scripture plenty of times in the past, but it was no longer in my current artillery. I am not perfect, but I *know* that I am the righteousness of God in Christ. This was exactly what I needed to speak over my son. I was getting worried because it had been a long while since he checked in, and he was not responding to my or his sister's texts.

"God," I pleaded, "Do not let my son die addicted to alcohol, alone, depressed, and miserable." Let him see the goodness of the Lord in the land of the living. (Psalm 27:13) *You* said that the seed of the righteous *shall* be delivered!" Whatever it takes, deliver him!" I believed that if my son were to die that he would awaken in heaven. He constantly prayed, repented, and pleaded with God for help. Given the opportunity, Jimmie would call upon God with his final breath.

The next week, while intoxicated, he plunged to the bottom of a steep flight of stairs, broke his neck, and was scheduled for emergency surgery. Sitting by his hospital bed, watching him go through DTs, wearing a cervical collar, I prayed. He awaited surgery. Surgery was delayed several days for low white blood cells, elevated blood pressure, and other complications. My nursing brain clicked and dangled images of my son spending the rest of his life paralyzed, wheelchair-bound, and dependent on others for his care.

I spoke to my director about medical leave. I informed my family that Jim would be moving in with us. My body tensed with anxiety at the thought of experiencing uncontrollable episodes of his rage. He struggled hard to control his anger while in my presence. The most he had mastered was fifteen minutes. Not long enough to live with me! Yes, he was always sorrowful afterward, but not before his anger inflicted emotional injuries and sometimes property damage.

This was even more trying because our country was experiencing a pandemic resulting from COVID-19. The world was cornered into lockdown. When first admitted to the hospital, it was business as usual. Within days, the world was scampering for toilet paper and hand sanitizer and afraid to touch anything or anyone. The hospital restrictions limited one symptom-free, mask-wearing visitor for ICU clients only. It was eerie pulling into the nearly empty parking lot when, just yesterday, I could barely find a parking space. I walked through bare waiting areas that are normally filled with families awaiting updates about those receiving surgery. He was in the ICU when his surgery was completed.

The surgeon reported, "The procedure will not heal the weakness resulting from the damage to his cervical spine. He hoped it would stabilize it and prevent further damage. "It is possible that he will need more surgery in the future and continue to experience some level of pain and weakness." I thanked God that though he experienced pain and was not 100% following surgery, he was not paralyzed.

Twenty-four hours after surgery, he was transferred to a step-down unit, and I was no longer able to sit at his bedside. While in and out of DTs, he was at the mercy of the medical staff to meet his needs in the absence of his family. I thank God for the excellent care he received during this time. He was offered the option of going to rehab before discharge. I advised him to take it, and he was transferred a few days later. "Mom, they are not doing therapy; everyone is confined to their rooms."

It was pointless for him to remain in this restricted rehab setting with no therapy. I asked the social worker to request a discharge order for him to be released into my care. I noticed that something was different about Jimmie over the past few days. I sensed this even before he transferred to rehab. When talking in person or on the phone, Jim was patient, kind, gentle, and understanding—this was an unexpected but welcomed change. Not normal…

"Must be the narcotics," I thought. Small irritants that would have caused him to end our conversations in the past abruptly went unmentioned. I wasn't sure if it was God or his incapacitated condition. I was grateful that he was walking and able to care for himself when released. I was concerned and did not want him to return to the upstairs apartment, where he landed at the bottom of the stairs, which could have proven fatal.

"I stood at the top of the stairs and looked at my body lying at the bottom." He later reported this while sharing his testimony during our joint Facebook video. God not only gave him a miracle but another chance at life!

COVID infections and death totals swept the nation during his stay with me. We engaged in family prayer and devotions every night for over a month. God did much during this time and completely restored our broken relationship. My book titled, "Forgiveness, the Antidote," was used for some of our devotional study and interaction. It shed insights on how to allow God to heal our hearts so that we could continue to move forward. We grieved the love we were deprived of sharing over the years while celebrating our new journey.

We ministered to others on social media sharing the power of forgiveness and God's ability to restore even the most hopeless situations. Many parents praying for their adult children using drugs, alcohol, or imprisoned shared that they were encouraged by our testimonies.

It felt like I was sleepwalking in a dream when I observed him throughout the day. I had to do double and triple-takes to realize—*this is real!* "God, you did it! You gave me back my son!" No one in the household experienced a single episode of Jim's unleashed anger. Jimmie shared how he wept and repented while lying in the hospital. He was loving, kind, gentle, and positive. Very pleasant to be around. I was sad when he decided to return to his apartment, and I truly miss him. If any man be in Christ, he is a new creature. The person I drove home from rehab, was not the same one the ambulance rushed to the hospital. Jimmie shared this about his transformation.

"I didn't try to wipe my tears while praying and asking God for help. I just let them roll down my face. I thank God for giving me another chance!" Jim's restoration is far beyond anything I ever could have asked, thought, or imagined.

The Bible says that the virtuous woman's children would rise and call her blessed. Mine all did—except Jim. "This one will *never* call you blessed, satan mocked over the years. This is just one of the many lies of satan that God has exposed. Jimmie and I treasure the moments we share. We have discovered that we enjoy the same foods, movies, and jokes. We end each interaction with, "I love you's." Most of all we share a love of praising and worshiping our God.

It is a joy to know that our family has another intercessor who has risen to decree the promises of God over our lives. The journey can be long and the battles intense, but God *is* Faithful. There is *hope* for our adult children. Yes, we get weary. Don't allow weariness to muzzle your mouth. Pronounce the blessings of God over their lives! The seed of the righteous shall be delivered! For the mouth of the Lord has spoken it!

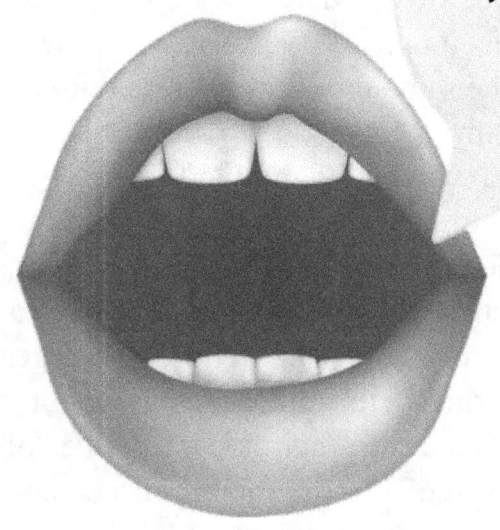

Delight yourself
In the Lord and He shall
Give you the desires of your
Heart.

Psalms 34:7

I DESIRE DECREES!

I DESIRE household salvation for my children's children, and my children's, children's children, and as many as the Lord our God shall call!

I DESIRE TRUTH in the inward parts!

I DESIRE You more than my necessary food!

I DESIRE You more than a mere mortal companion!

I DESIRE multiple streams of income!

I DESIRE to communicate with others with humility, boldness, confidence!

I DESIRE to walk in supernatural manifestation of the power of God with love, and compassion!

I DESIRE God to make the crooked places straight in every area of my life!

I DESIRE to live a life with an authentic presentation of my God and myself!

I DESIRE to be a blessing to the families of the earth!

I DESIRE my life to be visual evidence of the love and the goodness of God towards His people!

I DESIRE family generational curses to be broken on maternal/paternal sides of the family!

I DESIRE for my seed to be established in their destinies, purpose and identity in Christ!

I DESIRE for my Father, God to be well-pleased with my service!

I DESIRE to fulfill the plan of God for my life with love, joy, and pure motives!

I DESIRE fulfill Your plan and purpose for my life!

I DESIRE the heathen for my inheritance!

I DESIRE to leave a legacy of faith for future generations!

I DESIRE to be a blessing to the families of the earth!

I DESIRE to tread on scorpions and serpents!

I DESIRE God to show me great and mighty things that I know not of!

I DESIRE a clean heart and a right spirit!

MY I DESIRE DECREES!

_____

_____

_____

_____

_____

_____

_____

_____

_____

_____

_____

_____

_____

_____

_____

_____

_____

I

Thank
God!

HELP!

I dragged to my car with a migraine, heart palpitations, and weariness following a stress-filled workday. After cashing my check. I confronted the thirty-mile drive to pick up a friend from work. Clunk! After about ten miles, the back of my car collapsed onto the concrete. My car jerked and I wobbled it to the side of the express. Yep, a blowout! Flashes of my neighbor's warning me about my bald tire yesterday jolted my startled mind. I slumped against the steering wheel in remorse while beating myself in silence. "Why didn't I cancel this commitment after being warned my tire was bad!"

My father was a mechanic, but I knew zip about cars. The scorching sun and humidity intensified my headache and frustration. While lowering the window and activating the emergency blinkers, I prayed. Safety concerns flooded my mind. "God, I need help, not just anyone. Send one of your Servants."

Motorcycles, cars, and even police officers zoomed past. Some blew and waved laughing. "So cruel! I don't want your help anyway!" Tired, frustrated, and watching the lowering sun my prayers grew desperate. Locked inside the steaming vehicle with cracked windows, I sat feeling helpless. Nearly three hours passed. It felt unusual, people in this area were normally neighborly.

"Get out, go through the motions like you're changing a tire, and maybe someone will offer help." I took my thought's advice and stepped out of the car, jerked the trunk, and began an astute rummage like I was searching for something. Not a single car stopped. "Am I invisible!" I thought while climbing inside, locking doors, and activating the emergency flashers. Secured inside, I began wishing I was more like Doris, my tomboy sister who could rip apart a car and put it back together! My urgent petitions to God became draining.

Words from a past sermon replayed in my head. "Don't wait until God answers your prayers; thank Him for the help that is on the way!" It had been ten years since I attended church. God was dealing with my heart about returning, but as fast as He spoke, I hurled back flimsy excuses. For years, I was taught God doesn't hear a sinner's prayer. This belief caused my prayer activity to dwindle big time during this backslidden state. I acted right away on this memory.

"God, I am not going to say another prayer; thank You for the help that is *already* on the way!" I declared with rising confidence. An hour passed—*nothing happened!* Just before hopelessness swallowed my wavering faith, a car slowed and parked in front of mine. The driver walked to my car with a pleasant smile.

"Hello, looks like you need some help he spoke through my half-lowered window. I spent an hour figuring out which way to get back to you. I couldn't remember what exit you were on."

"Wow! Help *really* was on the way!" In minutes, my car was jacked, and he was ready to change the tire.

"Where's the lock for your hubcaps?"

Clueless, I thought, "Hubcaps have locks?" I never knew they had locks or even what one looked like. We searched everywhere as I grew angry for lacking such basic emergency roadside knowledge. He finally pulled it from beneath stuff in the glove compartment. Minutes later, he was done! It took longer to hunt down the lock than to change the tire!

Fatigued, hot, and annoyed after being stranded in the heat for over three hours. I offered heartfelt thanks. Home, here I come! I turned the ignition key with relief and excitement! Click, Click, Click! The emergency flashers drained my battery! My joy vanished, and disappointment claimed its space. "Now what? I don't want to hold this nice man up any longer. He might get frustrated, but it's going to be dark soon… Remember how long it took for just one person to stop?" "This mental debate ended in seconds.

I sprung the door and stepped out of the car with an apologetic expression. "More problems?" He spoke with patience and gentleness.

"Yes, dead battery."

"Do you have cables?"

"No." Another oversight that I slammed myself for at that moment.

He strolled a few yards alongside the highway looking from side to side in silence scanning the ground. I was puzzled. "I hoped to find a piece of wire or something to use." He explained while walking towards me. "Is there somewhere I can take you to call a tow truck?" This was *BCP—before cell phones.* I identified a nearby location. I gathered my purse from the seat and grabbed the envelope of money stashed beneath the floormat (I placed it there after the blowout). I prayed for safety while strolling beside him towards his car. My numbed body felt like it was moving in slow motion.

My memory rolled to a recent media release about a missing woman. Her abandoned car was discovered on the side of the road. "Has anyone seen this woman?" News anchors asked during repeated airings to solicit information from viewers. After two weeks—she was still missing without a word. A series of such abductions were blasted on the news from different states.

Riding next to him in the front seat, a similar news release began broadcasting in my head. Only this time, *I* was the missing victim. My photo features on the screen as the newscaster asks, "Has anyone seen this woman...? Her abandoned vehicle was found..."

"I've been watching oncoming traffic, and it's been slow." His words shattered my trance. He headed into the lane where oncoming traffic was merging onto the highway.

"I'm dead! This guy is a lunatic! I may have seen this done in action movies; high-speed chases executed in Hollywood fashion. Never in real life! My body became rigid with fear while trying to maintain a calm demeanor. He drove slowly as oncoming traffic blew to alert him that he was going the wrong way. He raised his hand politely, acknowledging the horrified drivers trying to warn him, smiled, and continued driving, acting like this was nothing unusual. I barely breathed. This freeway entrance finally ended on a familiar highway a few blocks from the place where I asked to be taken.

"Thank God!" I proclaimed as my helper drove into the restaurant's lot. I sighed as the weight of the day's venture began dropping. He maintained his kind and gentle demeanor until the end.

While expressing thanks and saying goodbye, I extended my hand, holding a crumpled twenty-dollar bill, saying, "Please accept this for your time and inconvenience." I initially hid the money from my cashed check in fear of robbery. By this time, I would have happily relinquished every dime; I just wanted to get home! I have since forgotten his name, but I'll never forget his kindness.

His piercing eyes locked with mine, and the quality of his voice changed. It was strange and reminded me of the scripture in Revelations 1:15, which describes a voice sounding like *the voice of many waters.* "No, take it and put it in church Sunday." This stranger had no way of knowing that I had strayed from church and God had been trying to get my attention. Then he added, "I'm just a *Servant of the Lord.*" These were the last words he spoke to me, and they penetrated my heart. These are the exact words I used in my prayer! The aftertaste of what had just transpired led me to believe this was no ordinary man.

God is Faithful and did exactly what I requested by sending one of His Servants. I did attend church that Sunday and placed twenty dollars in the offering. This was the beginning of healing my broken relationship with God.

71

When facing unknown seasons or waiting for answers to prayers this scenario serves as a reference. It reminds me to thank God for His answers and to continue to decree His word over my life—even *before* it manifests. Regardless of your circumstance, believe and thank God for the help that is already on the way. *It's true,* God moves in mysterious ways.

ONE HOUR

Prayer. We all need it! A minister shared; "many pray to do the work of the ministry envisioning a large, powerful platform. What they fail to understand is—the work of the ministry is— *prayer."* It is prayer that has sustained me and my family over the years and yes, sometimes it is difficult to engage.

"Thank You, Lord, for feeding me. I so appreciate You! Thank You, Lord, for helping me to find this! God bless this sister or that brother…" I talk to God throughout my day and involve Him in the minutest details of my life. If you were secretly filming me during these conversations, you would think I was experiencing full-blown hallucinations! I consider these activities prayer. Luke 18:1 says that we should always pray and not faint.

I enjoy conversing with God throughout the day. *But* there are levels in prayer. I need a set time for intentional, targeted, and focused prayer. Prayers fired at the kingdom of darkness like rapid-fire artillery. "I need you to pray one hour each day in the Spirit," I heard the Lord speak clearly. When walking with the Lord, you can sense when He is attempting to elevate you. You feel His pull, attempting to draw you closer. Yet this can only happen as we determine to align ourselves in obedience to His instructions and commit to spending more quality time in His presence.

During this season and the writing of this book, wearing a physical mask is yet mandated. Many are strutting both the visible mask and the invisible demonic muzzles. I struggled to follow this prayer directive but failed miserably. Don't get me wrong; there are seasons when I pray for hours while losing all awareness of time. I zip through my day declaring the promises of God. During these times, the only thing that matters is His presence. The presence of God has a way of arresting you, and even if you could leave—you have no desire to.

Other times, mustering a single prayer is like trying to extract a drop of water from the parched desert ground. This is where I was when I received this prayer directive. After minutes, my focus diverted, and I found myself engaged in other meaningless activities. Even making simple decrees seemed an invasive chore that I sought to escape. All the while satan's voice is whirling in your head. "Look at the state of the world! Do you think your prayers matter? What's the use of prayer anyway?" All the while terrified that you would arise and pray!

satan has a way of inducing temporary blindness to the mounting stack of answered prayers you *have* experienced. he deflects your attention to things you have been praying about for years—that has not been resolved. his efforts go into overdrive, doing everything possible to minimize our commitment to prayer. he creates a delusion in our minds until prayer becomes a routine, rhetoric, or a mere religious activity.

It is warfare to rise to the occasion of prayer while cornered by demonic forces. When summoned by the Holy Spirit to pray, I battle distractions and the temptation to gravitate toward fruitless activities. I hate this! I imagined the heaviness and disappointment Jesus must have felt while praying in the garden. Praying in agony and sweating blood. Did he feel a spark of hope believing that His disciples were nearby praying with Him?

Imagine Him discovering His sleeping disciples who had pledged to stand by Him through victory or defeat. Perhaps snores from their slumber greeted Him before he witnessed their sprawled bodies. "Could you not pray with me for one hour?" Our Savior, facing what He knew to be the greatest test of His ministry, would have felt comforted by one hour of prayer.

"Could you not pray with me for one hour?" This scripture echoes each time I fall asleep or engage in other actions luring me from this prayer commitment. One hour of prayer would have sufficed our Lord at the most critical time in His life. One hour of prayer must be more power-packed than we can ever imagine!

The Holy Spirit makes intercession for us. The Bible acknowledges that we do not know what to pray for. I love this because it's true; sometimes, I don't know where to begin in prayer. There are many outstanding needs such as— family, friends, church, the corruption in our nation, the devastation in the world—all deserving of our prayers. New issues emerge daily! I get overwhelmed.

God reassured me once that I don't need to worry and carry all these burdens as long as I pray what He places on my heart each day—He is pleased. He reassures that there are many others in the body praying. Are they? Or are they sleeping? Now I have this new instruction not only to pray for one hour but to pray in the Spirit.

Praying in the Spirit is a powerful activity and causes all kinds of things to occur in the spiritual realm. A woman shared how when she began to pray in the Spirit, she heard satan taunting. "Listen to you," he begins launching accusations. "If your husband hears you, he is going to know that you are just a hypocrite!" After pointing out her failures and flaws, she allows the demonic muzzle to be re-secured over her mouth. Praying in the Spirit is the pathway to freedom from the things satan uses to blackmail and hold us hostage. The one thing we know for sure about satan is he *IS A LIAR!* Yet we tend to allow his lies to crash our ears and barricade inside our minds, and then we become immobilized with fear and live our lives acting as if these lies are true.

I love praying in the Spirit! Sometimes, streams of profanity or other wretched thoughts pour through my mind while praying. This is satan's way of intruding to cause frustration and derail my prayer. Have you experienced this? It comes a time when we have to pause and discern that this is *NOT* me! It's coming straight from the pit of hell! Cast down these evil imaginations and *continue* praying. When we submit ourselves to God and resist the devil, he will flee! (James 4:7)

When God gives specific instructions to pray, it is for our protection. Disturbing dreams have disrupted my sleep on and off for several years. A different dream with the same troubling theme. I usually awaken feeling distressed and needing a moment to get grounded.

One morning, I woke livid with anger toward satan! "I'm tired of these stupid dreams!" Dreams purposed to fill me with despair and hopelessness. I knew they were diabolical. I determined that enough is enough! The next night, I experienced a breakthrough. 3 am, I engaged in a warfare prayer with the Holy Spirit leading the battle. As I write this chapter, I can say that I am once again experiencing His beloved sleep.

In my heart, I propose to develop the discipline of praying in the spirit an hour a day. Jeremiah 33:3 says, "Call upon me, and I shall show you great and mighty things that you know not of." This scripture is talking to you! The God of the universe is always inviting us into private chats. How amazing is that! The rewards of spending quality time with God is worth pursuing and overcoming *any* spiritual battle.

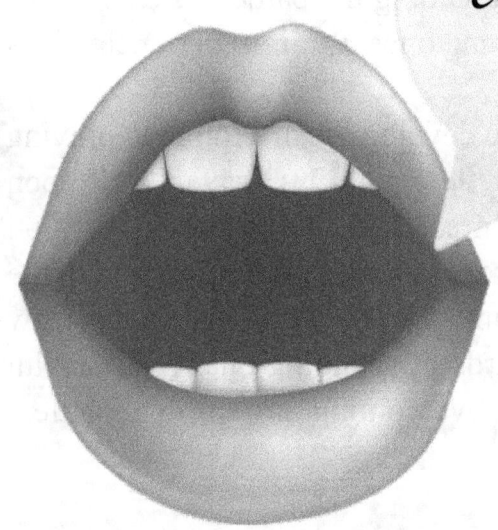

I THANK GOD DECREES!

I THANK God in EVERYTHING, for this is the
will of God concerning me!

I THANK God that He always causes me to
triumph!

I THANK God that He has given me everything that
pertains to life and godliness!

I THANK God for doing the exceeding, abundant,
and above all that I could ever ask or think!

I THANK God for preparing a table before me in the
presence of my enemies!

I THANK God for loving me with an everlasting love!

I THANK God for He is good and His mercy endureth
forever!

I THANK God for His amazing grace!

I THANK God for sudden, sweatless victories!

I THANK God for making the crooked places straight!

I THANK God for fortifying me!

I THANK God for teaching my hands to war!

I THANK God for making me an Ambassador for Christ!

I THANK God that I open my mouth wide and He fills it!

I THANK God that I have favor with God and men!

I THANK God that He restores my soul!

I THANK God that I ask, and I receive, I seek, and I find, I knock, and the door is opened!

I THANK God that He has given me the keys to the kingdom!

I THANK God that while I am yet calling, He answers!

I THANK God for miracles, suddenlies, acceleration, and the manifestation of answered prayers!

I THANK God that all the promises of God are yes. I thank God that the Spirit brings all things to my remembrance!

I THANK God for renewed strength

I THANK God for He is good and His mercy endureth forever!

I THANK God for eternal life!

MY I THANK GOD DECREES!

_____

_____

_____

_____

_____

_____

_____

_____

_____

_____

_____

_____

_____

_____

_____

_____

_____

CLOSING PRAYER

If you have felt muzzled by the enemy, as a prophetic act, say this prayer and go through the motions of removing the muzzle and casting it aside. I did—it works.

God, I thank you for sending your word and delivering it to me. I repent for aligning my thoughts, words, and actions with the lies of satan. I cancel every idle word that I have spoken in agreement with the power of darkness.

I plead the Blood of Jesus over my heart, mind, soul, and mouth. I pray that the fire of the Holy Spirit destroys every satanic stronghold, and every demonic muzzle stripped, freeing my mouth to declare your word over my life.

Thank you for giving me decreeing power. Open the eyes of my understanding to the importance of winning the war of releasing your decrees over family, job, finances, health, relationships, and everything that pertains to me.

Amen

Decree!

Decree!

Decree!

Decree!

Decree!

Decree!

Decree!

Decree! The word of God over yourself!

Decree! The word of God over your family!

Decree! The word of god over the lost!

Decree! The word of god over the sick!

Decree! The Word of God over your relationships!

Decree! The word of God over your finances!

Decree! The word of God over your city!

Decree! The word of God over our leaders!

Decree! The word of God over the Body of Christ!

Decree! The word of God over our nation!

Decree! The word of God over Israel!

Decree! The word of God over our world!

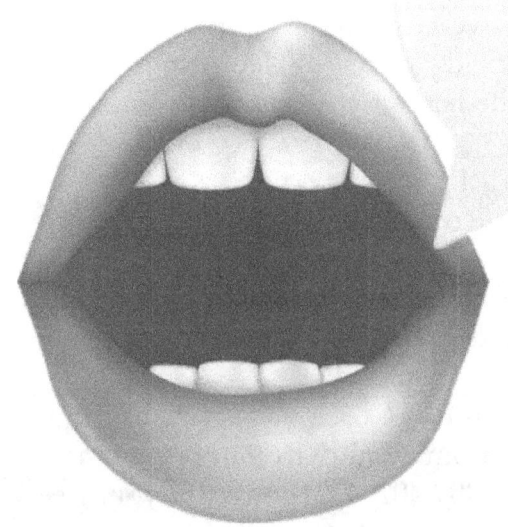

AUTHOR'S NOTE

Whether ministering to others as speakers, writers, or through other giftings it is necessary to decree the word of God over our lives. God has given us the Holy Spirit to partner with to help us in this endeavor. If you listen, Holy Spirit will whisper empowering words to speak over your life for any and every situation.

God knew that we would get weary during this human experience but admonished us not to get weary in *well-doing*. Even while standing amidst the barren fields of unfulfilled expectations, through eyes of faith behold the harvest you anticipate springing forth.

Though others spoke into my life over the years, my journey as an author and writing coach began when I said so. We are living in a season when God has placed a supernatural demand on His people to write. Many are overwhelmed by this urgent assignment.

Is that you? My I Am a Writer NOW! Coaching Service has from start to finish launched many from writers to authors. Email: jeri@iamawriternow.com or call **989 402-4721** today for your free consultation.

ABOUT THE AUTHOR

Minister Jeri has learned to observe and respect the power of words. She makes every effort to impart this reverence unto others. She has witnessed God's response to declarations that she's made over her life, time and time again.

Jeri is an Author, Speaker, Songwriter, and Writing Coach. Any success that Jeri has experienced she attributes to learning to not only *believing* but *saying* what God says.,

Arise today!

Unto a new place

of

Prayer, Praise, Promise,

Provision

&

Prosperity

Using the Power

of

SAYING SO!

CONTACT INFORMATION
THANKS FOR
READING
SAY SO!

YOUR AMAZON

OR

FACEBOOK REVIEW

IS

APPRECIATED!

OTHER TITLES
BY
JERI DARBY

Bit.ly/Jeribooks also available on Amazon

Forgiveness, the Antidote

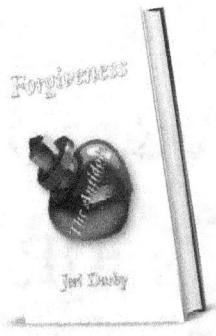

Stepping Stones   **Paso A Paso**

Reflections for Singles
(THESE ALSO AVAILABLE IN SPANISH)

Poetic Meditatio from theThrone

Seasoned for this Season,

Reflections for
Seasoned Singles Singles

SOON TO BE RELEASED!

ACKNOWLEDGMENTS

God, I thank you for everyone that invested in pre-ordering my book. I pray that you will bless the works of their hands and cause them to prosper and be in health...

Jeannie Castell-Morris, Author
Book: A Cry for Help, Finally Free!
Email: jeannie2609@gmail.com
989 392-4911

Columbus Williams Sr., Author
The Gift, Echoes of Poetry
Available on Amazon
Email: Columbuswilliams180@gmail.com

Juliann Deadrick & Mary J. Holcolm
Children's Book Authors
The "It's Me, Poxey!" Series, Coming Soon!
Email: itsmepoxey@gmail.com

Congratulations Mom! Johnnie Darby (Son) 😊
I love and miss you, I thank God for you every day!
Watching what God is doing in your life is amazing!
Thanks, for all the love, prayers & support you show us!

Divine Grace Ministry
Apostle Bobby & Prophetess Mary Johnson
3271 E. Atherton, Burton MI 48529
Website: divinegraceministries.org

Dr. Sandra Peoples
Publishing Coach & Consultant
Sandranpeoples.com
Facebook.com/Sandra peoples

Dr. Cint Gilstrap
Book: Stolen (Shattered Years of My Childhood)
Rescue, Refine, Restore, Coaching & Counseling LLC
Website: www.cintgilstrapministries.com

Maneka Day, Author
Book: Ragged Wrinkles
Facebook: Maneka Day
Phone or Inbox to Order: 989 332-7079

Esther Clark, Author
Book: A Brick House
Available on Amazon
queenestherclark@gmail.com

Joseph Brown, (Grandson) ☺
Congratulations! I know your book is going to
Inspire millions of people,
And change many lives for the better.

Zipporah M. Shropshire
Legal Shield
989 992-2163
www.zshropshire.info

Patricia Hampton
Iron Sharpens Iron
What a Joy to share a Journey of Faith
With You!

Shontaye Bibbs, The Playmaker
A Woman's Playbook
Website: http://www.AWomansPlaybook.com
Email: AWomansPlaybook@yahoo.com

Patricia Qualls, Author
Book: The Perfect Pastor's Wife & Other Fairy Tales
Email: patriciaqualls0317@yahoo.com
Facebook: Patricia Jones Qualls

Lisa Faizan (Sister) ☺
The Business Mindset Coach
Facebook: Lisa Faizan
Email: lisafaizanllc@gmail.com

Stevetta Temple, Author
Book: A Broken Heart Made Whole
Bit.ly/brokenheartmadewhole
Stevetta.temple@yahoo.com

Kaneisha Woodhouse, Author
Book: Into His Secret Place
Available on Amazon
kaneishawoodhouse@gmail.com

In Loving Memory, Alberta Culpper, Author (Other Mom) ☺
Book: More Poetic Reflections
Available on Amazon
Email: eculpepper@mmhia.com

Congratulations Mom, Yolonda Brown (Daughter) ☺
Reading & Editing "Say So!" provided me with practical &
powerful affirmations to apply to my daily life.
You are an amazing writer and my favorite author!

Cheryl Walker, Author
Book: Living Purpose-Full (Devotional for purpose seekers)
Available on Amazon
Email: Cwalkercv2010@icloud.com

Apostle James & Prophetess Leona Glenn
Center of Attraction Outreach Church
4375 S. Washington Rd.
Website: www.centerofattraction.org

Mary Moss, Divinely Designed LLC
Website: school.divinelydesigned.us
Lminktr.ee/themarymoss
momoss1956@gmail.com

Brennan Jackson (Grandson) ☺
Grandma, you have been faithful, giving up sleep and free time,
to be a voice to God's sheep. I love you! Continue to bless
others with your videos and books!

Mercy Myles-Jenkins, Author, Coach
Rebuild, Reset, Recovery 7 Steps to Spiritual Abuse Recovery
www.AuthorsMercyMylesJenkins.com
Follow me on Facebook: Mercy Myles-Jenkins

Julie Raymond, Author, Coach
Much is Expected Life Coaching
Facebook: Much is Expected Life Coaching
Email: muchisexpectedllc@gmail.com

JoAnn Long, Author
Healing Of A Mother's Heart
Facebook: JoAnn Long
Jlong657@gmail.com

Eric Culpepper, CEO/Principle Agent (Honorary Brother) ☺
Website: www.mmhia.com
Email: eculpepper@mmhia.com
Toll Free: 1 844-533-7432

Kelly Joy Brown, Brand Ambassador & CEO
"I Make My Moves in Silence Collection
Website: www.imakemymovesinsilence.com
IG Instagram-@imakemymovesinsilence

Rudell Foster, Jeri, your book on Forgiveness
Helped to heal my heart! I couldn't put it down!
I am excited to read your new title, Say So!
I anticipate more inner healing. Thanks...

Andrea Gonzales, Author & Impact Life Coach
Book: Gimme15
Website: angonzales.com
Email: andreamotivations@gmail.com

Jimmie Brown (Son) ☺
Not only is she the Author of this amazing book,
And many others, she is also my Mom.
Love you Mom!

Pastor Wesley Allen, Author
Church: Redeemed Ministries
Book: Oneness Within
Email: wewesleyallen@aol.com

Anna Hernandez, Author
Book: Look at the Future and Laugh!
Facebook: Eternal Impact Media Ministry
Email: arhernand01@gmail.com

Jasmyne Rhianna Brown (Granddaughter) ☺

Granny, I look forward to reading your book!
You always know what to say and when to say it.
Congrats! More to come!

Ivy Crudup, Author

Book: Misunderstood, Battling Fear & Anxiety
Available on Amazon!
Facebook: Ivy Crudup

Deborah Templeton, Author

Book: Silent Cries During Hurricane Seasons
Facebook: D Templeton
Email: templetondeborah173@gmail.com

Carlos Salamanca

https://fineartamerica.com/profiles/1-carlos-salamanca

Huni Wilson, Author

Book: When A Man Preys
Website: whenamanpreys.weebly.com
Facebook: Huni J'dore

Desmond Bibbs, (Son) Proud of you Mom! ☺

You demonstrated Servant Leadership for me all of my life.
I celebrate your embarking upon success with your books,
while sharing your life-changing testimonies with the world!

Jerome Buckley, Publisher-Advertise/Promote Your Business

The Michigan Banner News
Website: www.themichiganbanner.com
Email: publisher022@gmail.com

Marilyn Schafer, Children's Author

Book: The Eaglet Who Was Afraid to Fly
Coming to Amazon Soon!
Email: nursemarilyn52@gmail.com

Jayla Nicole Brown (Granddaughter) ☺

Another one down! Many more to go!
I am so proud of you!
Love you, Grandma...

India Pernell, Author
Books: Mae Flowers, Poetry Meadows, Indy's The Ugly Prince
Available on Amazon
pernellindia@gmail.com

Diamond Nicholson (Granddaughter) ☺
My grandmother is my biggest inspiration. She is strong and independent and has helped many. Congratulations! Granny I wish you the best! I love you...

Annette Carnes, Author
Books: Healing A Broken Heart & The Armor of Light
Available on Amazon
Email: annette4god@gmail.com

Candess Brown (Granddaughter) ☺
What else could you give a woman that's been touched by God! Your light shines majestically in this world.
I love you, Granny! Congratulations!

Lavarne White
Jeri, you are inspirational to others that have unfinished writing projects. Keep up the good work and continue to encourage your readers!

Cleotha Brown (Brother) ☺
Congratulations, it is amazing when you can follow your dreams. I always believed in you! I wish ongoing future success!

Shelley Smith (Sister) ☺
I love the unique way you construct words when writing. Proud of you! Continue pressing towards your goal of completing 100 books! I am cheering for you!

www.ingramcontent.com/pod-product-compliance
Lightning Source LLC
Chambersburg PA
CBHW071021120626
46546CB00003B/1182